Happiness

RULES!

by

Judy MacDonnell

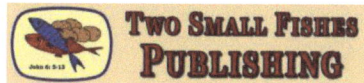

TWO SMALL FISHES PUBLISHING

Happiness *RULES!*

(To view more of Judy MacDonnell's work, please visit: www.judyspatch.com)

Art work by Lindo C. Maningo Jr.

Cover Art by Laura Shinn

(To view more of Laura Shinn's works or cover designs, visit: www.laurashinn.com)

ISBN-13: 978-0980836868
ISBN-10: 0980836867

DEDICATION

To all the children of the
world.

Ten rules God gave,

no more, no less —

these ten short rules

for happiness:

1

Don't worship anything
but *Me*.

I am the Lord,

I set you free!

2

Images and idols

do nothing for you,

Make *Me* first

in all you do.

3

To use My Name

is to call on Me,

so never use it

carelessly.

4

Six days I made

for work and play;

the *seventh* is

My holy day.

5

Respect the parents
who gave you birth,
and you'll live long
upon the Earth.

6

Don't hurt or kill;

be kind and true.

Do as you'd want

to be done to you.

7

Marriage is a gift

for two –

just you for one

and one for you.

8

Don't take someone

else's stuff,

though you haven't

got enough.

9

Be truthful till
the day you die,
and never, ever
tell a lie.

10

Be happy with the

things you've got.

Don't wish for

someone else's lot.

Loving God and

others too,

brings happiness

to me and you!

www.ingramcontent.com/pod-product-compliance
Lightning Source LLC
Chambersburg PA
CBHW042121040426

42449CB00003B/138